Begging the Question

Also by Jane Williams
Other Lives (Ginninderra Press)
The Last Tourist (Five Islands Press)
Outside Temple Boundaries (Five Islands Press)
Some Towns, Wagtail 73 (Picaro Press)

Jane Williams
Begging the Question

Acknowledgements

I am grateful to the editors of the following publications in which poems in this collection first appeared (some in slightly different form): *Arabesques Review* (Algeria), *The Age*, *Australian Reader*, *Blue Dog*, *Blue Giraffe*, *Blue Pepper*, *Black Market Press* 18 (New Zealand), *Cordite*, *The Orange Room Review* (USA), *Poet's Republic*, *The Stinging Fly* (Ireland), *Takahe* (New Zealand), *The Tasmanian Times*, *Verandah*, *Wet Ink*.

Some were broadcast on *Writers Radio* (Radio Adelaide).

'Arrow' won the 2006 Wet Ink Poetry Competition.

'A difficult woman' was highly commended in the 2006 Wet ink Poetry Competition.

'Mount Wellington' was commissioned as part of the 2004 Mountain Festival and commended in the 2006 Henry Kendall Poetry Award.

'Girls I grew up with' was commended in the 2006 Henry Kendall Poetry Award.

I am also grateful to the Australia Council for the Arts and to Arts Tasmania for grants which assisted in the completion of this book.

Begging the Question
ISBN 978 1 74027 475 3
Copyright © text Jane Williams 2008
Cover image: Emily Kelly

First published 2008
Reprinted 2017

GINNINDERRA PRESS
PO Box 3461 Port Adelaide 5015
www.ginninderrapress.com.au

Contents

Churches of the developed world	7
Arrow	8
Some towns	9
Green means stop	10
Shrinking	11
First sight	12
Bully	13
During a discussion on retirement homes	14
Class act	15
Visiting poet	16
Applause	17
Bone	18
Just Visiting	19
After lovers	20
Project bookends	21
Symmetry illusions	22
The land of just right	23
Begging the question	24
Fortune	25
Deviations on home	26
Surprised by joy	27
Days of hope	28
Windows	29
Girlfriends	30
This is not a political poem	31
On receiving a letter from an ex-lover	32
Business as usual	33
The real McCoy	34
Groupie	35
Attachments	36

Source material	37
Like a gang	38
Just dolphins	39
No one looks the part any more	40
Death by drowning	41
In the wee hours	42
The relative thickness of blood	43
Common ground	44
Girls I grew up with	45
Peddling poetry	46
The unwritten law of living	47
A difficult woman	48
As you tell it	49
After the funeral	50
Small talk	51
Cause	52
Mount Wellington	53
Poem on the edge	54
11 memos for the 21st century	55

Churches of the developed world

(a partly found poem)

to light a candle
drop any coin into the slot
(more coins may be required
for longer prayers)

on medical advice
communion is to be made by
receiving the bread only
(salivation is to be kept
to a minimum)

not in use
the alms box owing to recent
forced removal of padlocks
(bag checks now operate
in this church)

under electronic surveillance
you
(and you and you and you…)

Arrow

this is how it happens you are exactly who you think you are
someone who's been around long enough to know the world
is spinning without needing to feel it when out of the blue
carbon copy day a young woman half-skipping toward you
waving her long arms and shouting hey happy new year happy
solstice all piercings and dreadlocks when she gets close enough
she says sorry she thought you were someone else someone
she once knew someone named arrow and all the rest of the way
home you wonder what freedoms a name like that a name like
arrow might have meant for a woman like you perhaps a market stall
or self-defence classes a degree in emotional intelligence hitch-hiking
alone at night eyes like star charts amazon women warrior friends
dropping in for morning tea and all your dreams flying out like
arrows from the scar that marks the spot where a breast used to be
this is how it happens how you find yourself suddenly airborne
and spinning through that first tunnel of light

Some towns

there are still to be found in some towns even the progressive ones
eager to be born again if only on paper the ones that aspire
to a mall and two cinemas an all you can eat with free tokens
for the pokies and an all weather playground for the kiddies
the ones whose hospitality trainees are just now learning how to fake
six different kinds of real coffee why chicken and fish don't belong
on the vegetarian menu why (soy) sausages and burgers do
the ones with plans for a well being centre a pain clinic
a women's movement a men's movement and a twelve-step program
for everything else
there are still to be found in some towns those shop owners who say
to those shoplifters you only had to ask (and mean it)
fry-up breakfasts made in ignorance but with love
family doctors trusted to deliver the next generation
and neighbours who know enough to know timing changes everything
when to call the cops when to mind your own and when exactly when
to put the kettle on

Green means stop

wearing a traffic light green t-shirt
standing in the middle of the road
trying to stop cars for a hand out
creating irony but nothing edible
as the day warps into art's sake
and only the odd tourist
catches shock like a cold
feeling culturally confused
this is Hobart – Tasmania…right?
the locals know her name
has passed its use-by date
even writing about her in the present tense
is risky business

Shrinking

my daughters who have reached
their optimum height tell me
I am shrinking

more and more
I look up to them

we joke about how soon
they will have to watch their step

learn how to bake tiny loaves of bread
pour thimbles full of wine
and listen very very carefully

one day
if we are to have our order of things
that is that they outlive me and we
all outlive the cat

I will disappear entirely
from their view from their touch
there is nothing to prepare us for this

I role-model compassion
and comic relief
in equal measure

sometimes out late at night
testing the elasticity
of the thread between us
I sneak back early
hoping to catch them
rehearsing their lines

don't worry (exaggerated hand-patting)
she'll come home when she's hungry

First sight

you look like a young man again when
talking about the sales assistant from the tip shop
the one with eyes like a welsh accent or a meteorite
or the first time a circus came to town
these are my words not yours
you can manage only sighs
and…*oh! the eyes! the eyes…*
the colour (shall we say?) of alchemy
your dicky heart revamped between
the china and the tupperware
chipped and buckled
into pre-loved resignation
but a purchase made leaves no excuse
not to avert your gaze
and anyway you know what feast
memory makes of just one taste
and something else some distant siren warning
that if you drink too long from such exacting portals
the world might shed its skin of all things mortal

Bully

drunk gun among pet rabbits
belly full of stolen lunches
at school bully king pin never gets hit
out in the workforce weapons change
a callused fist becomes a smooth tongue
bully learns which word does the job
of a bruise or a break
how to measure blows by the book
but on careless days when all that weight
goes to the head bully slack-mouthed
swaggers
out of the office into the playground
kiss my arse he dares
and god help us some of us do

During a discussion on retirement homes

he said
even if they call it
a village
let me grow garlic
fruitless tomatoes
sleep in my wet suit
I'd rather live
off the coast line
eating raw fish heads
he said
even if I can't remember
why not
tell you the time is right
that I want to be around
people my own age
don't you dare
he said
not quite foaming at the mouth
believe a word of it

Class act

you disappeared
without a trace leaving nothing but the memory
of the final act no smoke screens trapdoors
nothing but a winged prayer up your sleeve
simply one second elevated centre stage
in a halo of spotlight and the next   not
wild applause and whisperings of how it might be done
but no one true believer really wanting the answer
your biggest fans receiving exquisite postcards
in the form of visions
celestial stamps winking in the terrestrial dawn
suggesting anyone
anyone with half a brain can pull a rabbit from a hat

Visiting poet

wears a dragon fly in one ear
when she opens her mouth
haiku form on her tongue
natural as pearls
she reads about bodies
of water and conversations
with women about men
between poems she calls out
spontaneous greetings
to people in the audience
as if surprised to find
she is not alone
her right hand holds steady
the weight of words in transit
her left hand is sometimes
preoccupied
rearranging the flowers
on the fabric of her skirt
but mostly it stations itself
between her hip and the small
of her back
as if she is with child
and all the world their oyster

Applause

you are hurrying along to work or the gym or maybe you are running
away from home
the hour is early and only the very secure or displaced are up and about
you are walking alongside a row of unassuming inner city houses
when sudden unmistakable applause emanates from one of them
you stop to be sure and sure enough a minute later there it is again
applause!
heavy curtains drawn across the window of the house keep you safe
from being discovered as you stand riveted by hope
as you count down the seconds and are not disappointed
most baffling of all in between each round of applause   silence
perhaps the smallest child in a large family has just learned how to flip
the breakfast pancakes
or a magician's apprentice is practising disappearing in front of the mirror
spurred on by intermittent canned clapping
you may never know but this morning at least you will walk tall in the light
of imagination where every attempt is deserving of a standing ovation

Bone

here where the dreaming girl unmakes herself
in the image of false idols waking becomes a curse
a place stepmothers lead you to then leave
she spots blood to find her way back too many times

learns the sick skin is admired and ribs are counted
like money each eye a glass bead reflecting
an oasis a vision of ever afters

weightless she believes the body
seeking a pure vent of way will be like origami
with every fold the possibility of a wing

in the final phase it is a concave world
miser appetite hoarding all knowledge of food
for the baby-fat winter that never comes

here where meagre shadows cast themselves
a stone   a stain   a still thing
the tongue whittles kisses to bee stings
as the first bone cries out refusing to be dressed

Just Visiting

in this part of the hospital I want a name tag
that reads *Visitor* in clear clean-cut letters
because everything I know and don't know
about electric shock treatment I learnt from
one flew over the cuckoo's nest
and while you don't look like your brains have been fried
or the lights have gone out I am afraid
to look too deeply I am afraid of finding you
here where you make your own blades from coke cans
until someone in authority twigs
and you are drinking purified water from a foam cup
playing pool shooting hoops like normal is as normal does
when she's not looking you point out the Virgin Mary
paranoid in the corner reminding me we are all clichés
after the fact that there is no clear clean cut line separating
those of us who are living it from those of us who are just
visiting and when I think of the scissors in the sink stained
with the real thing I know I would have been useless
what good would it have done to yell shark no matter
how accurate the analogy metaphor isn't rescue

After lovers

I

at night it is the bogong moths
at my window
frenzied as monks in a mosh pit
seduced by artificial light
by morning it is the pink robin
breast displayed like a sacred heart
announcing death or a miracle
between these two my own wings
beating as if treading water
against the deep end of sleep
I pray for amnesia and dream of you

II

when we say we were never lovers
the lie divides itself between us
like an only child who must be believed
because there is no other
still
to show I mean business I cut
my hair because it belonged to you
my mouth from your mouth
my name from your name
do not touch myself in my hour of need
without you
I am learning how to breathe

Project bookends

even though the year is 2007
and the woodwork teacher is a woman
an intelligent beauty with man hands
and this is Australia
and the project is Bookends
one of the girls still manages
to soften the wood
into bouquets of flowering love hearts
and one of the boys
carving the likeness
of Osama bin Laden
AK-47   key to the city
is primed and ready

Symmetry illusions

sometimes a white flower will take form behind closed eyes each petal visible and ed
in deepest pink vibrating in a spotlight of wind in the centre of a still black forest
do we think if we tidy up around the edges the eye of the storm will look kindly on

I

evening things up revealing
corners/edges
a single stone bench in a spotlight of sun
the roots of an old pine
he is pruning and raking and filling in time
whistling a soft shoe a lullaby
with one hand he drags a giant plastic bag
lumpy/lifelike
in the other cut flowers arrange him

II

bent forward under the weight of premonition
the woman running her voice straining
beyond recognition
the man's knees give way
his fists break open like accidents
a neighbour's window swallows the image whole

III

everywhere blooms struggle to hold their place
life patterns itself
against black rain and knocking
to be let back in
a practised hand from the inside
counts out the minutes like lashes

The land of just right

in the land of just right every body has its fill
nothing is too big small hot cold high or low
not a chiselled cheekbone to be found
nor a tweakable cheek nor belly's round
tabloids pay homage to the perfectly average
and though some heads remain overblown
being virtually empty there is no unseemly
falling over
no one dreams or desires outside the square
there is no suffering or exaltation of any kind
the ties of mediocrity be the ties that bind
in the land of just right the dark night of the soul
is as unheard of as a crime of passion or the song
of solomon or finger painting or donating blood…

Begging the question

who worries over this woman
fingering *you are my sunshine*
on the piano accordion
squat as an invalid's breakfast tray
above her outsized lap
track suited against the swank
of the commonwealth bank
when she reaches the end
please don't take
my sunshine away
she knows to start over
hour after hour
this music by numbers
this empty chocolate box
open for business
its heart-shaped lid
inviting payment for services
and begging the question

Fortune

manfred is translating
the cartography of my hands
it's what he does
into lucrative predictions
of buying and selling
he doesn't say what
of a woman putting her foot down
great healing powers he whispers
but what mother doesn't know that
and its flip side I don't say
biting my tongue
remembering how my best friend's
angora rabbit ate her young
you'll live he concludes
to eighty-seven
it's what I want to hear but
the shine in my eyes is blinding
the spring in my step fraught
I cross the first street without looking

Deviations on home

concrete

waking with some cold kerb at your hip but lucky
a saint vinnie's food voucher buys a steak sandwich and you
almost grin the whole day away the imagined aftertaste
of some cheap love drug beaded on your soul

nylon

in a two-man tent inventing ways to keep the cold out
and the dreams in at the supermarket you only steal what you need
the thin green between your world and theirs foretelling grander thefts
what it would be like that first night in jail just to see if you belonged

aluminium

you pick the egg-shaped caravan facing the 24-hour servo
away from the amenities building
and when it rains hard the small window above the collapsible table
with its tropical jungle print curtain shows the blinking lights
of semi trailers like an old circus movie and you think you show promise
balancing on your high wire practising your next move

fibro

finally a bedsitter and you even make a friend to guarantor a small loan
to make it feel more like home you say then use the money to buy
red lace curtains some weapons give yourself an exotic name hide from the sha

Surprised by joy

and why not? nothing we can plan for
a mistake to think we can replicate
some once upon a happier time
because that was then and joy like love can
be at the worst of times the best
of unexpected things
it might have something to do
with that extra ray of vitamin D we
instinctively turn to
to soak up the madness from our eyes
when we roll the crooked dice
when we're told do not pass go
do not collect reward hormones
all pleasure centres closed until further notice
call it serotonin or endorphin
call it God's plan or the agnostic's concession
whatever the science whatever the faith
there joy waits unconditionally in the wings
like a marionette with itchy feet
or a bored altar girl for something to break
                and set her free

Days of hope

in the all-night bottle shop the underage couple
insubstantial as shadow puppets in profile
standing side by side hands and feet touching
two paper-chain dolls dressed in neon
cut off from the rest and intent on being
forever in love
wanting to celebrate the mere idea of it
eyes shining with every new thing
loose change flash backing to mixed lolly days
asking hope filled in silver-lined whispers
for something they can mix with lemonade

Windows

super heroes and poets take to their ledges
fantastically metaphorically sometimes literally

reminding us that rescue involves a leap of faith
from one kind life into another

two trains idle side by side two strangers look out
lock on and hold just long enough

for the question to take shape for hearts to skip beats
they never knew they had

open or closed anyone can see through to the other side
and then there's the eyes being what we hope they are…

yes – as a point of entry and exit I think all things considered
I prefer a window to a door

Girlfriends

diamond street girl white brick with arches landscaped garden
gold mercedes and doris the pure-bred bull terrier
walking the wee hours in flannelette and torch beam
up the steep tar bicycles grow wings on
left turn where the road unmakes itself
past the englishman's house with the too tall daughter
he thinks of as regal who wishes she were invisible
past the two-storey brick-veneer teenager with twins
past all things rumoured walnut-faced and whispering
over paling fence and dandelion lawn and into the dream life
of silver street girl green weatherboard with mission brown trim
orange kingswood station wagon and skipper the labrador cross

This is not a political poem

about Banda Aceh and inappropriate tsunami
aid like boxes of breast implants wigs and fur coats
the fight for East Timorese independence the subsequent
donation of buses too wide for the narrow roads of Dili
too expensive to run for longer than a joy ride left to rot
this is not a political poem
about one size fits all campaign speeches
promises self-fulfilling as a five o'clock shadow
suits climbing the ladder corporate or social
what does it matter divining water from rock
this is not a political poem
about the price of petrol or a family holiday to Alpha Centauri
ski slope cheek bones bee sting lips the colour of poverty
the weight of guilt by omission
my enemy's enemy is my friend and what's mine is yours
but don't worry this is not a political poem
I don't write political poetry

On receiving a letter from an ex-lover

even though
it had contained only
forwarded mail
I kept the envelope
astonished to find
after all this time
all it took was my name
in his handwriting
and I was seeing again
the alluring cursive
shape of love
how the *j* curved back into itself
like a figure skater
the way the *e* trailed off as if
to be continued…

Business as usual

I'm a five-dollar fare hardly worth the smile
I throw into the bargain
but he's not I suspect so much in it for the tips
too old to be a taxi driver doing the graveyard shift
and we're not so different I think out at night
trying to squeeze a little more life out of life
half joking about driving beyond destinations
the road a never-ending promise
faithful as the moon or a good dog
willing to follow us anywhere no strings attached
we share a moment of wishful thinking
his foot hesitating between the brake and the gas
my mind losing its grip on all things frugal
then the meter stops ticking over
and it's back to the business of living as usual

The real McCoy

young and lucky enough
grief on the face of it
other people's lot
and acts of god well out
of your sympathetic hands
but when you hear about a certain
beautiful young man
one you went to school with
jack of all hearts the real McCoy
loved by every girl
and the least likely of boys
when you hear how he became
motorist and road statistic
on the same luckless day
your own ballooning heart
becomes a land mine
you must tip toe around
and what was once the neutral
territory of your faith
quakes ever so slightly
beneath your carefree tread
as you wake from childhood ether
to the stuff of blood and bone
if he can die so can I
alone alone alone

Groupie

today I fall in love
with the woman at the bus stop
I fall in love with her sky blue earplugs
and lolly pink backpack
I fall in love with her half closed eyes
suggesting a foot in heaven's door
I fall in love with the way she sways
like a professional mourner
or an amateur drunk
dangerously close to the edge
of being discovered but mostly
I fall in love with the way she sings
too loudly off-key
not knowing half the words not caring
I wait for the bus I want to be there
join in
when the windows shatter their applause

Attachments

periodically I lose what I become too precious about

that indian scarf I wore for definition disappeared
from my pale neck on a mountain walk
I didn't know it was gone until I'd descended
sheltered from blurred edges and a cryptic sun

a ring I couldn't take my eyes off
silver emblazoned with a golden spiral
every conversation every ulterior move
lead with that hand dizzying me into blind spots
I would never wholly return from

frequently I lose my sense of direction
and have to play tourist to find my way home

I have lost the moment the hour the day
and once in another tongue the will to live

I lost you of course but that was written

after dreaming I lose my place in the waking world
everywhere I look strangers in a strange land

I am always startled to find someone knows my name

Source material

the sleeping body is its own home
modest as the page before the poem
one vanity a silver chain
has worked its way up from the neck
through itinerant dreaming
to settle and glint like a sun-kissed
snail trail across unkissable lips

hobo   vagrant   bum

woken to observe the observer
would such a man be content
to snap at well timed heels
or would he (who could blame him?)
go for the jugular
where life and art coagulate
halfway between head and heart

Like a gang

so much so that
the general public
part before them
nothing miraculous
just caution
in the 21st century
mid afternoon
in an Australian city
just kids
passing around
a toy cap-gun
taking turns firing
into the crowd
a few people startle
suck air and swear
the world's gone mad
mouths hung open
long enough
for it to mean something
but nobody screams
and there's no blood
none of the real fear
that in some circles
passes for respect
not their circle
not yet
and by the time it reaches
the hands of the leader
the novelty has almost
worn off

Just dolphins

once it was enough to be king
for the turn of a tide
make castles out of sand
race waves back to shore
and pocket seashells
for inland friends
these days you take the obligatory
recycled family holiday
there are plans for a boat
another kid maybe but basically
it's the same old same old
beach combing between cans of beer
light enough to keep your heart
ticking over your feet on the ground
you scan the ocean with eyes restless
as prison tower searchlights
call out now and then
to lagging family members
that you think you see something…
something…then shake your head
surrender upturned palms
as you realise they're just dolphins
again
no loch ness monsters here
each year you wonder what it will take
a shark sighting
might get the blood pumping
a beached whale
something sink your teeth into

No one looks the part any more

not the man with the white cane and black sunglasses
taking the arm of a pretty young woman saying
you don't mind do you stepping up and into the tram
clinging to her long after she's guided him
to the two seats vacated quickly enough
under the assumption that he's blind and they're together
not the pre-pubescent private-school boy small for his age
red hair flaming against all wishes searching
with sticky bun fingers through his pockets for the bus fare
he just spent on his first sugar fix for the day begging change
from the skinhead with fuck spelt correctly on his t-shirt
not the middle-aged woman adeptly applied makeup
respectable skirt length and sensible shoes pushing
a shopping trolley full of the debris of other people's lives
wolf whistling and winking at no one in particular
not the cyclist approaching a breakfast crowd
dining al fresco suddenly
tipping himself from his bike and into the arms
of a bewildered businessman who rises to break the fall
because by now people are watching thinking perhaps
accidents happen or a heart attack
but on closer inspection two men holding each other
as though it's the last warm thing they expect from life

Death by drowning

I never met
my mother's second cousin
know her only in the context
of one stark image
designer clothes folded
and stacked into a pile
neat as the edges
of an arranged marriage
right down to the bra and knickers
smalls my grandmother
would have called them
I imagine the whole affair
topped off with impractical shoes
and a real gold watch
she walked into the ocean
and never looked back
now and then beach combing
I am struck
by the inevitability of such an image
a woman turning away from
or toward herself
all the trappings in the end
useless as a velvet-lined coffin

In the wee hours

otherwise faithfuls whisper wrong names into the ears of lovers
who keep breathing but do not stir
do not give the impression they heard a word out of place

a child wakes sits bolt upright in bed but still asleep
and screams run for your lives the house is on fire

a woman dreaming of the cliff edge of her marriage
clings with renewed hope to her side of the bed

insomniacs try to run out of things to count

a grandmother of six plugs herself in to her own theme music
runs a hot scented bath introduces herself to herself
as the Queen of Sheba slipping cat-like between lives

drug induced sleepers dream dreams they won't remember
but will go about their day
all day checking their pockets certain they've lost their keys

a father watches the clock tick over curfew tries not to remember
what he got up to at that age calls his daughter's name
to come / heel / stay   as if this   could ever bring her home

and the body becomes just that as the soul struggles to equal
the simple sum of subtracting a dead weight from a live one

The relative thickness of blood

you are holidaying with your estranged
son who is suddenly eighteen
well mannered computer literate
you take him to a baseball game and
he doesn't complain
over dinner you realise his voice
has become too deep to compete with
that the memory of when it broke
does not belong to you
he tells you he gave up marijuana
exactly twenty days ago
as for the tobacco he's cutting down
saves money by rolling his own
when you ask about goals he tells you
move out of home repeat year twelve
make his mark in IT
there was a girlfriend it was serious
that was the problem
you think how you never knew
your own father how a little gene-
alogical digging revealed three marriages
a cast-iron liver no interest in kids
you know he's got it all this boy
man son of yours the looks the smarts
the heart it's a hat trick you tell him
because sport is a safe bet when
what you really mean is something about
the relative thickness of blood about re
inventing yourself then being true

Common ground

the man in the open-plan
phone box is speaking
a language as different
from my own
as heart is from stone
but with his free hand
he builds on the air
layers of meaning
and as I pass I see
the shape of familiar words
you   me   now
the way they hold themselves
like cornerstones
marking out common ground

Girls I grew up with

she had white hair and eye lashes and a pet rabbit
that could talk (to her)
we rode hand-me-down bikes to vacant allotments
where we drank home-made lemonade
and coloured each other in with miniature cosmetics
passion purple and orange tango
courtesy of our avon-calling mothers
I mouthed the word albino like a secret too delicate
to speak or swallow
her name was julie but to me she will always be alice

from the italian who once swore at her father
in my presence in english a word I'd never used
I learned about bluff
he puffed up like an amateur wrestler
she tossed her botticelli curls in my direction

pale-skinned with blue-black hair and disney red lips
smart enough to corner the market for the family business
the butcher's daughter warned me
look back and you could be turned to sawdust

my namesake was all elbows and knees like me only taller
tall enough for basket ball but she wanted to be a ballerina
once as we leaned into each other imitating gossip
she let me touch a newly formed breast then
asked for a cup of tea to settle her nerves last I heard
she was making wedding dresses for a living
but I remember when we were witches doubled over
our bubbling futures how we smiled benignly at non-believers
each time we died and were born again

Peddling poetry

the woman in the gift shop explains she sells more tangible accessible craft toffee you
can get your teeth into huggable sweaters g-rated calendars teaspoons and tea towels
coasters but no ashtrays not these days she takes the book turns it this way and that a
if it is an abstract painting unsure which way is the right way up she has a look that
could be saying something about poems that don't even rhyme being a waste of God
given space not to mention time *wouldn't buy poetry m'self* she admits when pressed
wouldn't read it though I s'pose this proposed a little cautiously *some might*
she doesn't go on to suggest the cardinal sin that others yet again may even write it
and I wish she'd ask me what it does so I can tell her the right poem
can take your breath away return it sevenfold inflating parts of your brain
you never knew you had it can shake your faith or just as likely restore it
knock the chip from your shoulder bring a dogma to heel trigger cries of joy that leave
your enemies wondering what it is they're missing out on wrench from you a howling
that sends your lover running to hide all the knives it can leave you silent so silent you
begin to hear things you never heard before the sound of your mother wanting you
just the way you are the sound an angel makes when falling the sound love makes
when it isn't being asked to qualify itself the sound of the desire for war
spontaneously combusting the right poem can make you believe and forsaking
all others for the rest of your days follow wherever it may lead

The unwritten law of living

everything worth anything
must break
it is the unwritten law
of living

day
bread
vows
egg

any favoured piece
of crockery or glassware
how long did you think
it would last

one quarter
of our body's bones
are in our feet
mind your step the signs read
but feet soldier on oblivious

of all the rules worth breaking
do not fraternise…

no x-ray will show the number
of breaks a heart can outlive
such knowledge it is rumoured
could kill us

A difficult woman

you tell me you are a difficult woman
this is how you introduce yourself

do you mean like a book
that is difficult to read because it is written
in a language other than…

or the lid of a jam jar
difficult to open
before it is loosened

do you mean like a poem
that is difficult to warm to
because it mirrors coldly

or a sailor's knot
difficult to untie without experience
or fingernails or teeth

do you mean like a new religion
that is difficult to believe in
because it tells the truth

or a promise
difficult to keep when you fall in love
with someone else

you tell me you are a difficult woman
this is how you introduce yourself

As you tell it

absolution as you tell it
is the exhilarating thing
about becoming
a middle-aged catholic
the visual I get
is of you leaving
the church after your first
confession
face and arms thrown skyward
one knee bent one foot elevated
in 1940s hollywood kiss mode
whatever light there was that day
insinuating itself under your very skin
as you strike your iconic pose
advertising the best deal
in what money could never buy

After the funeral

released from the weight
of the word
railings pews kneeling pads
still hold a little heat
on such a day the flesh is weak
the spirit also
but everywhere signs of struggle
a litter of damp tissue
tossed in an irony of mock confetti
as if such a day could make
or break any god's faith
black and gold canine hairs
imbedded in reserved
front row carpet
the abject loyalty
of man's best friend
permitted on such a day inside
his master's father's house
frankincense and myrrh
mask the beginning
of a grief it will hurt to let go of
midsummer sun filtered through
stained glass turns the altar
into a jigsaw of light and dark
a garden view window
bears the mute protest
of one child's nose and hand prints
as if to say on such a day the world
lies in wait but outside all of it outside

Small talk

raining I offer *but not cold* I am making small talk with the bottle
shop attendant because to not do so diminishes us both
yeah he says nonplussed then with more enthusiasm *yeeaah*
and I swear it's at this point he finds himself
deep in meteorological thought as he makes a shy connection
between the weather and philosophy *it's the illoosion* he explains
what makes you think it's cold just coz it's raining
and I can't help wondering how many shifts he's been waiting
to use the word *illoosion* because the way he says it
gives it the ring of a word that's been pent up biding its time
loosening inhibitions the way a drink or two can unfulfilled
by self talk aching for audience appreciation reciprocation
sometimes I have the same feeling about the word love only in reverse
the way we use and abuse it loving most of what we only
have a passing like for *love the hair dress shoes thanks love
no worries love go on love be a love you've got to love her him
this place* ad nauseam until *I love you* just doesn't have the same
authentic ring to it as the word *illoosion* when newly discovered

Cause

there's a man who wakes our street
to that hour between witching and dawn
most used for dying and for being born
he paces and moans like he already knows
who will be taken and who will be left alone
those of us who dare   untuck a sleep-warm arm
raise a dream-filled head and peek from safe houses
at the shape of such a man but it is the hour
and the tone that warn we roll over keep listening
some of us urging him on and on
some of us double-checking locks and the breathing
of sleeping children some of us remembering
where the bullets are hidden our trigger fingers
twitching like guilt between the sheets some of us
think we understand and loved ones have to hold us
back from running out into the night ready to join
our rusty voice to his desperate for a cause

Mount Wellington
(a pilgrim's guide)

take with you plenty of water and one mustard seed of faith
pause at notice boards detailing the botanical names for Mother
and Child and Man Fern
take a moment to visualise this kind of harmony in your own life
locate the hunting ground that echoes *you take one of ours*
we'll times it by five dead or alive dead or alive
circle head bowed as many times as it takes forgive yourself but
never forget
tell a story about a woman without title who marched to the beat
of her own drum two weeks before Lady Franklin (upup upup)
only looking down from the top to guess which part of the Derwent
had washed all motive from the body of her dead husband
learn how to brew sassafras beer dig tunnel vision
camouflage access paths
see yourself too drunk to care – then care
un name this mountain seven times climbing downward
through a selection of Australian histories the best of British
and French intent to arrive at the original Aboriginal namings
do not trust the vote to democracy (note you will need to make this climb
as an amateur in order to maximise full learning potential)
having found your way in offer a simple non denominational prayer
remembering the full heart doesn't ask for much –
a hut to call its own air clean enough to shape breath
wordless nights spent re discovering tracks to other hearts
and how best to maintain them
in return a promise
to resist all temptation to climb the mountain just because it is there

Poem on the edge

the poem on the edge wingless forcing you back into yourself
into older neglected selves open and dangerous as the parts
selective memory leave out moving you away from everything
else the poem on the edge childless not a poem you can tell
your husband or your lover about a stranger maybe
a poem in which conviction becomes less urgent where
invisible ink is used to mark the line between eccentricity
and madness and religion is as unanswerable
as the distant thud of the blunt end of a crow bar or a forgotten
land mine going off somewhere you tell yourself the poem
on the edge godless is somebody else's business will write itself
out of harm out of harm's way

11 memos for the 21st century

I consume I am consumed

A computer is not a library is not a tree

Make the time to find the time

Sugar-coated anything goes

My promises are full of promise

How are you is not a trick question

Keep the wolf from the door by inviting him in

The moon hasn't left me

When we fall we land on common ground

Welcome home

It's all good it's all good it's all good

www.ingramcontent.com/pod-product-compliance
Lightning Source LLC
Chambersburg PA
CBHW062204100526
44589CB00014B/1942